PICTURING SCOTLAND

MORAY

NESS PUBLISHING

2 A panoramic view of Lossiemouth beach and the River Lossie estuary.

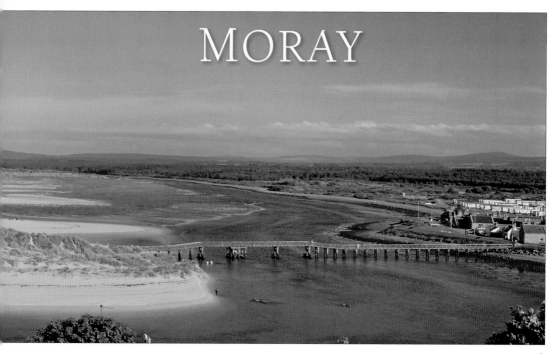

MORAY

Welcome to Moray! Part one: from mountain to sea

The modern-day county of Moray encompasses as wide a variety of scenery and depth of history as any part of Scotland. The boundary changes of 1974 saw it absorb the southern part of neighbouring Banffshire and this greatly expanded the 'new' county's geographical range. Thanks to this re-organisation, the south-western boundary of Moray passes through the Cairngorms summits of Cairn Gorm and Ben Macdui (second highest mountain in Britain). From this 1220m/4000ft plateau, Moray sweeps down Strath Avon and Glen Livet to glorious Speyside, world-renowned for its salmon fishing and malt whisky.

Moray also lost some territory to the same boundary changes, its former south-western corner being taken into the Highland Region. This included the town of Grantown-on-Spey, so in acknowledgement of its recent past and to allow inclusion of more of Speyside, this book will stretch a point and visit that area too. Also, since the first edition was published, and to the delight of the residents of Old Banffshire, the branding of *Historic Banffshire* has been created and applied to the relevant areas, highlighted by roadside signs.

As the county unfolds from the mountains to the sea, it embraces rich farmland that produces

Moray begins here! The county's western boundary runs through the summits of Cairn Gorm and Ben Macdui, forming an arc around chilly Loch Avon, seen here.

an abundance of crops, including the top-quality barley needed by the distilleries. The richness of the land has meant that Moray has been home to humankind for at least four millennia. The Picts ('painted people') have left dramatic evidence of their occupancy of the region: one of the most magnificent Pictish standing stones in Europe has been re-erected in Forres. Standing over 6m/20ft tall, Sueno's Stone was unearthed in 1726 and is estimated to have been carved in the 9th or 10th century. The name 'Moray' can be traced back to the 10th or 11th century, when it related to a much larger region ruled by a Gaelic-speaking dynasty, the best-known member of which was the infamous Macbeth, king of Scots from 1040 to 1057.

Elgin is the county town of Moray and location of many places of interest that reflect its long history. King David I (r. 1124-1153) granted Elgin royal burgh status; in 1224 it became the seat of the Bishop of Moray. The Cathedral, although a ruin, is one of the finest examples of medieval architecture in Scotland. Castle remnants can still be seen on Lady Hill and the town centre boasts a fine array of houses that reflect the styles of successive eras.

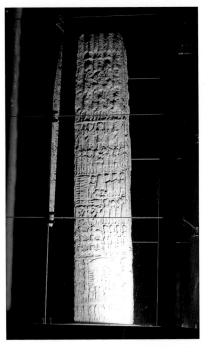

Sueno's Stone, floodlit.

The varied canvas of Moray is completed by its coastal strip that offers a wide variety of towns and villages. Most of these have their origins in the fishing industry, which is still active in some of them. Lossiemouth's magnificent beaches are a match for any seaside rival and so extensive that they are never crowded. The Moray Firth micro-climate extends its benevolent influence to this part of the coast and the waters of the firth are home to dolphins, seals and many species of seabirds. A very important part of the landscape and the economy is RAF Lossiemouth, under threat of closure at the time of writing. As a small token of support for the Base, a photo of one of their Tornado aircraft appears on p.1, positioned so as to introduce this edition.

So for residents and visitors alike, Moray provides something for everyone. The aim of this book is to give a taste of that variety and so encourage exploration, from mountain tops to seaside rocks – happy venturing!

Ornamental drinking fountain in the village of Tomintoul. 7

8   Founded in 1824 by George Smith, The Glenlivet Distillery is the home of one of the world's most famous malt whisky brands and is open to visitors for tours and tastings. It is one of eight distilleries

that form the Malt Whisky Trail, the other members of which will be indicated by (MWT) where they
appear in this book.

10 The village of Tomintoul, on the edge of the Glenlivet Crown Estate and in the Cairngorms foothills, is the highest village in the Highlands at around 355m/1160ft.

Moray has a share in Scotland's skiing industry at the *Lecht 2090*, as the road from Tomintoul passes 11 this ski and snowboard centre, located up in the hills on the border with Aberdeenshire.

12 Coming down Glenlivet, near the village of Tomnavoulin, it looks as though 'Daisy' is about to get a soaking from the approaching storm.

Further down Glen Livet by the B9008 is the Old Bridge of Livet. As built, it spanned the river in **13** three arches, one of which was washed away in the floods of 1829.

14 Attractively laid out Grantown-on-Spey, built to the plan of Sir James Grant, used to be in Moray and is the westernmost point in this book. This is the north end of The Square.

The Revack estate is just outside Grantown. Set in 350 acres of outstanding scenery with a walled garden, **15**
ornamental lochans and trails to explore, this picture captures the woodland beauty of the estate.

16 Ballindalloch is one of the most beautiful and renowned castles in Scotland. Known as the Pearl of the North, it is located in the heart of Speyside, near to many famous whisky distilleries.

A much loved family home, Ballindalloch is one of the few privately owned castles to have been lived in continuously by its original family. The Macpherson-Grants have resided there since 1546.

18 Left: the old Bridge of Avon, across the road from Ballindalloch Post Office. Right: the former railway viaduct at Ballindalloch now forms part of the Speyside Way.

The Speyside Way long-distance walk stretches 65 miles from Aviemore to Buckie on the Moray coast **19** (see p.86). It uses sections of the former Speyside railway, as here at Tamdhu (formerly Knockando) station.

20 Cardhu Distillery (MWT) at Knockando was established officially in 1824. It is the only malt distillery pioneered by a woman. The picture emphasises the link between barley and whisky.

On the opposite side of the Spey near Marypark, Glenfarclas (meaning 'valley of the green grass' **21** in Gaelic) Distillery has the largest stills on Speyside. This is its Visitor Centre.

22 Outside of the Cairngorms, Ben Rinnes is the highest hill in Moray at 840m/2755ft. Pictured in the depths of winter, the summit is away to the left …

… from which magnificent views can be enjoyed, in this instance by the author's daughter. **23**
Ben Rinnes is not a demanding climb, taking about an hour-and-a-half at a modest pace.

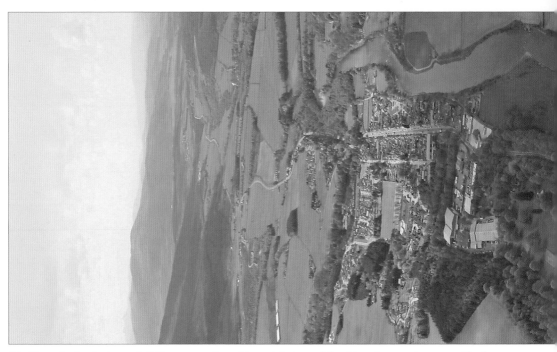

24 Turn the book through 90° to appreciate this aerial view of the River Spey as it passes Aberlour. It shows the neat plan to which the village was built. The group of large buildings is the HQ of

Walkers, the famous shortbread manufacturer. The picture on p.28 is looking along this stretch of the river from top to bottom.

26 Across the Spey from Ben Rinnes, over on the northern side of the strath, we come to the pleasing village of Archiestown, which was established 250 years ago.

Winters on Speyside are frequently harsh, as this February view of Archiestown shows. **27**
Ben Rinnes is in the distance.

28 The Spey between Aberlour and Craigellachie, a view which sums up Speyside: the river wrapped in the wooded hills with arable and livestock farming on its banks.

An autumn scene looking north-east across the village of Charlestown of Aberlour with **29** Ben Aigan (471m/1540ft) in the distance.

30 Aberlour Church of Scotland kirk. The settlement grew on the site of the church and well dedicated to Saint Drostan, and was developed in 1812 by Charles Grant of Wester Elchies.

The next village down river from Aberlour is Craigellachie, from where this precariously taken view **31** from above Telford's bridge shows Speyside at its summer best.

32 Along with the eight distilleries, the Speyside Cooperage (just outside Craigellachie on the Dufftown road) is the ninth venue on the Malt Whisky Trail.

A few miles further along Speyside is the village of Rothes, home of the Glen Grant Distillery (MWT), **33** seen here from the slopes of Ben Aigan across the valley.

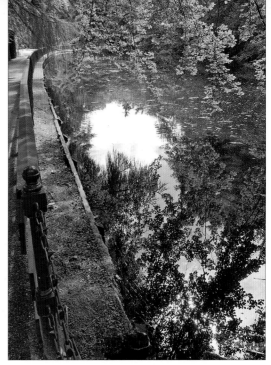

34 The Glen Grant Distillery (MWT) is noted for its fine gardens as well as its excellent whisky. Left: the burn (stream) that provides the distillery's water source. Right: the distillery pond.

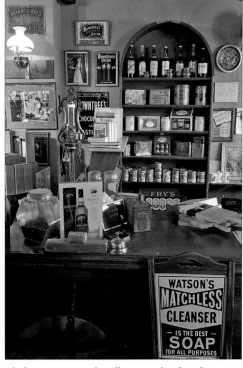

Exterior and interior views of Baxter's Museum Shop in Fochabers, a Speyside village north of Rothes. **35**

36 Fochabers village centre. Prior to the founding of the present village in 1776, the old township of Fochabers stood a short distance to the north, within the grounds of Gordon Castle.

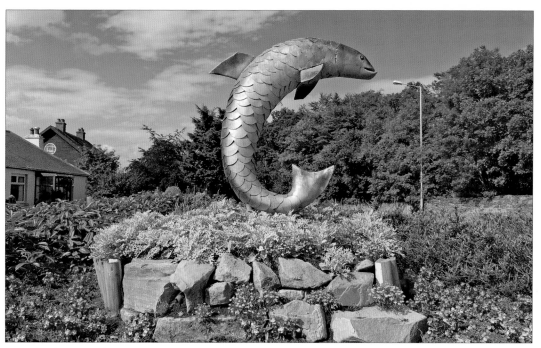

This leaping salmon sculpture greets visitors to Fochabers as they enter the village from the east. **37**
The Spey is one of Scotland's greatest salmon-fishing rivers.

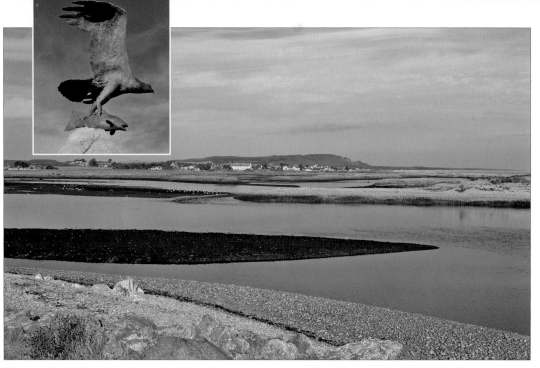

38 And finally the River Spey flows into the sea here at Spey Bay, 98 miles from its source in the Monadhliath Mountains. Inset: a fine sculpture of an osprey at Spey Bay.

The Spey flows into the outer Moray Firth, well known for its Bottlenose Dolphins. 39
The Whale & Dolphin Conservation Society has a visitor centre at Spey Bay.

40 From its position on the Cluny Hills above Grant Park in Forres, the top of Nelson's Tower gives fine views in all directions, like this one of Findhorn Bay and village to the north of Forres.

42 Brodie Castle is near Moray's western border, close to Forres. This fine 16th-century tower house is packed with enough art and antiques to keep connoisseurs happy all day!

The Findhorn river, pictured here at Logie, south of Forres, is rated by some as Scotland's most beautiful river.

44 Logie Steading, in its tranquil, park-like setting, provides visitors with a place for both relaxation and exercise – browse the shops, walk along the Findhorn to Randolph's Leap or enjoy the gardens.

Left: Logie's Longhorn cattle, the breed that originally made British beef famous, are one of the **45** oldest traditional breeds. Right: Logie House stands above the walled garden.

46 Just outside Forres, Dallas Dhu Historic Distillery (MWT) is an industrial museum perfectly maintained in working order. This unique time capsule is in the care of Historic Scotland.

Left: Forres has been a Royal Burgh Town since about 1140. This is Tolbooth Street. Right: The 70ft **47** Nelson's Tower was erected in 1806 in celebration of Lord Nelson's victories.

48 Forres is well known for its floral sculptures and is 5-times winner of Britain in Bloom. Some of these make a magnificent display here in Grant Park.

Left: the upper section of Forres Tolbooth, completed in 1849. Right: the Market Cross, **49** built in 1844, incorporates the base of an earlier, 17th century, cross.

50 St Laurence's Church, built 1904-1906. Of the many fine buildings in Forres, this is perhaps the most impressive. The interior is worthy of inspection too.

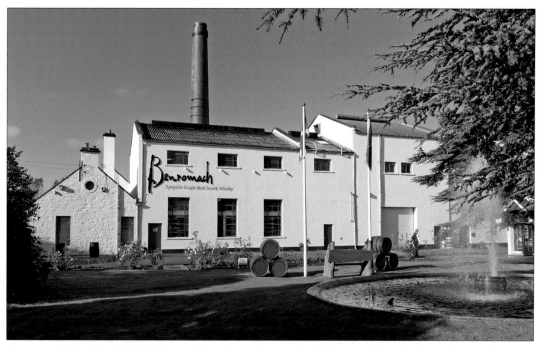

Benromach Distillery (MWT) is located on the northern edge of Forres. Although the smallest working **51** distillery in the Speyside area, it produces 150,000 – 250,000 litres of spirit per year.

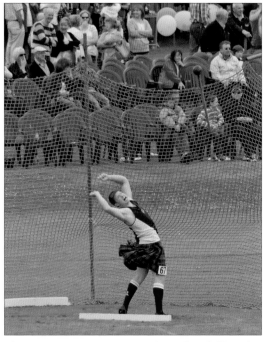

52 Forres Highland Games are held annually. Among the many events are Tossing the Caber (left) and Hammer Throwing (right). Pipe bands also march and play – see p.96.

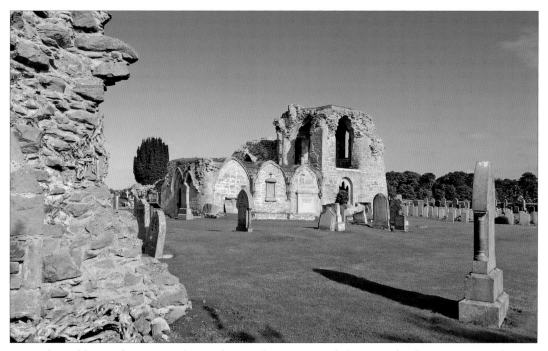

Kinloss Abbey is about two miles north-east of Forres. Founded in 1150 by the Cistercian Order, **53** it became one of the most influential monasteries in Scotland until its demise in 1560.

54 Compared with the picture on pp.40-41, this view gives a very different impression of Findhorn Bay, a popular location for sailing boats of many kinds.

The former fishing village of Findhorn, four miles from Forres, is nowadays home to the Findhorn **55** Foundation, a thriving holistic community and eco-village. This view is near the village centre.

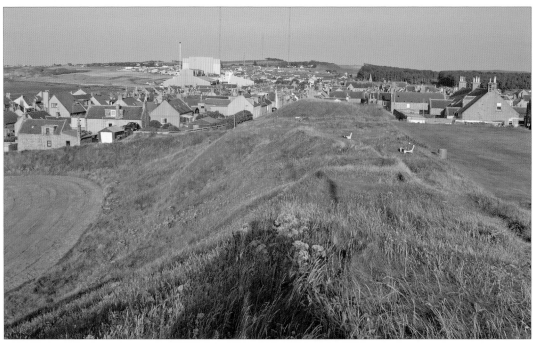

56 Going east from Findhorn we come to Burghead. This headland was once 'The biggest Iron Age fort in Britain', a Pictish stronghold from the 4th to 7th centuries. Pictured: remaining earthworks.

Burghead harbour still sees a certain amount of fishing activity. The nearby Visitor Centre has displays that illustrate and interpret the Pictish Fort.

58 Another short step eastwards and we come to the pretty seaside village of Hopeman. It is noted for its flair for decoration such as that applied to these beach huts. Inset: a ship weathervane.

And here is the reason for those beach huts: Hopeman's lovely east beach. This is the rockier side, **59** but the west beach is sandy.

60 A short distance inland from Hopeman stands Duffus Castle, the original seat of the De Moravia (Moray) family. One of the finest examples of a 12th-century motte and bailey castle in Scotland.

Located in the village of Duffus, Gordonstoun was founded in 1933 by Dr Kurt Hahn. Today's School has all the facilities necessary to give it a lead in independent education in the 21st century.

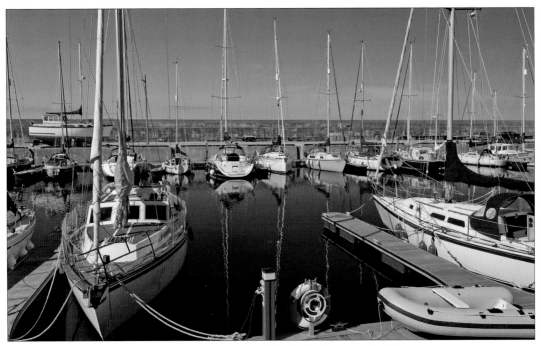

62 Lossiemouth is Moray's main seaside town, established at the mouth of the River Lossie as a seaport for Elgin. Its harbour has become a marina for pleasure craft.

The buildings on Pitgaveny Quay were built as warehouses for goods going through the port but **63** now serve other purposes, such as housing the Fisheries & Community Museum.

64 Lossiemouth is an excellent base for coastal activities such as fishing, sailing, wildlife watching or just enjoying the soft sandy beach and the dunes.

Pluscarden Abbey is a few miles west of Elgin. Founded in 1230, it is the only medieval monastery **65** in Britain still inhabited by monks and being used for its original purpose. Visitors are welcome.

66 Glen Moray (MWT) has been distilling single malt whisky since 1897. On the western outskirts of Elgin, it is open to visitors for tours and tastings.

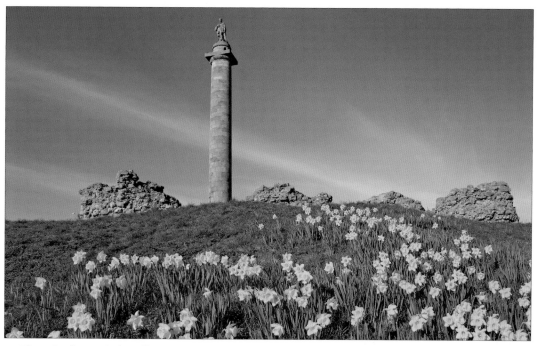

Elgin Castle, on Lady Hill, was a stronghold at a very early date and became a royal fortress in the **67** 12th century. Some remains can still be seen at the top of the hill.

68 Left: the monument on Lady Hill was erected in 1839 to the memory of the fifth Duke of Gordon. Right: St Giles' Church, built between 1825 and 1828, seen from the east.

Elgin town centre at Christmas is brilliantly illuminated, the lights adding new aspects to the **69** fountain and St Giles' Church. In daylight its many architectural styles can be appreciated.

70 On the left is a well-preserved townhouse built in 1694 which later became Braco's banking house. The Italianate building on the right was built in 1843 to house Elgin's excellent museum.

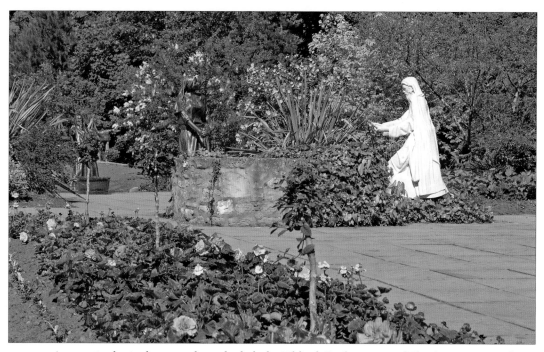

Appropriately sited next to the cathedral, the Biblical Garden is one of Elgin's more unusual attractions. Biblical scenes are recreated and all 110 plants mentioned in the Bible are featured.

72 On the left is the remnant of the town house founded by the Bishops of Moray. The 15th-century stone, defensible L-plan building possesses some pleasing architectural features. It was probably the manse of the Cathedral Precentor. On the right stands the west end of the Cathedral itself.

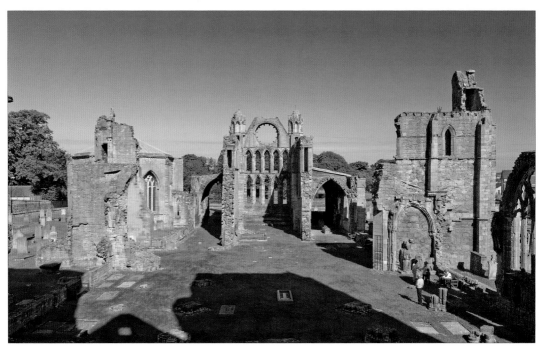

74 The remains of Elgin Cathedral, viewed from the west-end towers. Its many outstanding features include the country's finest octagonal chapter house, partly visible on the left.

Early morning light bathes the eastern elevation of Elgin Cathedral, seen here from across the **75** River Lossie. The cathedral was established in 1224.

76 Elgin's Cooper Park was gifted to the town by George Cooper in 1903.

Independently run since 1797, Johnston's has been making beautiful knitwear, clothing and accessories from the most luxurious wools known to man for over two centuries.

78 Just north of Elgin is Spynie Palace, residence of the Bishops of Moray for five centuries. Inset: this corbel in the Great Hall once supported the roof, now long gone.

Glenfiddich Distillery (MWT), just outside Dufftown. It is little changed since 1886, when **79** William Grant and his nine children built the Distillery with their bare hands!

80 Balvenie Castle, Dufftown, was originally the seat of the powerful Comyn earls of Buchan. It is an enclosure castle with a massive curtain wall, now in the care of Historic Scotland.

Dufftown was founded in 1817 by James Duff, 4th Earl of Fife, and is a typical planned town of the 81 area with the main streets being laid out in the shape of a cross.

82 Auchindoun Castle stands in splendid but strategic isolation in the hills south of Dufftown. It is thought to have been built by Thomas Cochrane, architect of James III, around 1480.

The market town of Keith straddles the Isla river. Left: a Keith & Dufftown preserved railway train at **83** Keith Town station. Right: Keith War Memorial.

84 Strathisla Distillery (MWT) goes way back to 1786, although it was not until the 1870s that this name was applied. Its annual capacity is 2.4 million litres of spirit.

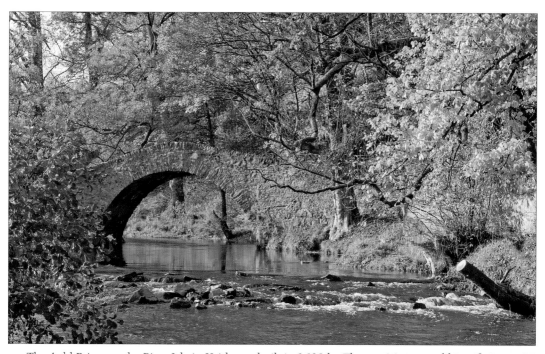

The Auld Brig over the River Isla in Keith was built in 1609 by Thomas Murray and his wife Janet **85** Lindsay, reputedly in memory of their son who drowned while trying to cross the river.

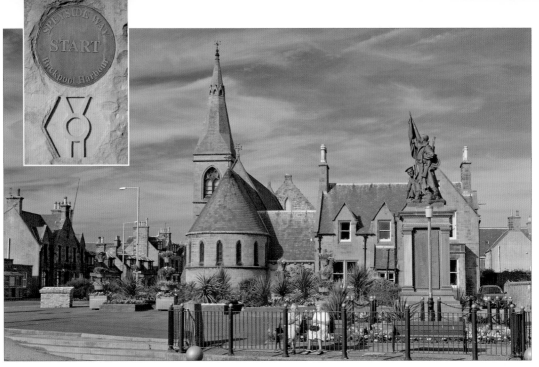

86 Buckie was the largest town in the old county of Banff and is one of the largest in Moray. This is Cluny Square. Inset: the Speyside Way starts in the neighbouring community of Buckpool.

Buckie's Cluny Harbour was completed in 1880; lifeboats have been launched here for over **87** 145 years. The shipyard builds and repairs lifeboats like the one in the picture.

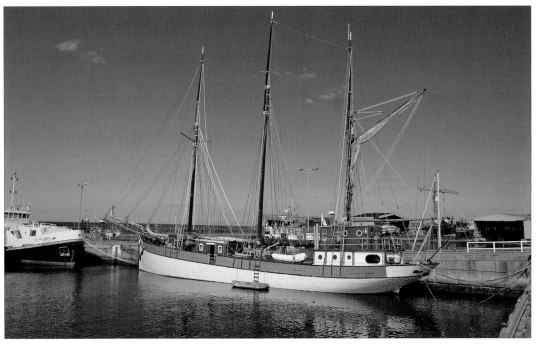

88 The fine old sailing ship *Regina Caelis* berthed in Buckie harbour.

A few miles east of Buckie is Findochty, a particularly attractive coastal village. It is an ancient **89** settlement, referred to as far back as the mid 10th century.

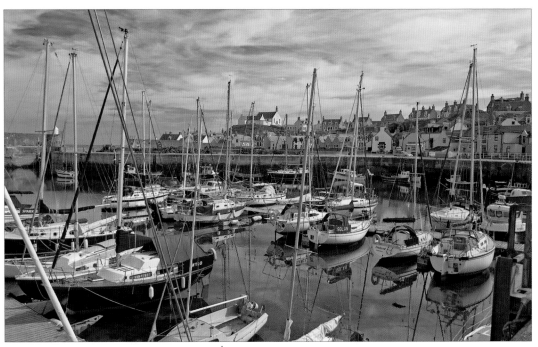

90 Findochty (pronounced Fin-ech-tay) harbour, in some ways like others in the county, and yet offering a scene that is unique.

This aerial view of Portknockie, the next village east, shows that it is a well-planned village, **91** laid out as neatly as the landscape allows.

92 The Bow Fiddle Rock is Portknockie's most visited attraction, but the village as a whole deserves exploration.

The pleasing town of Cullen is last stop on this journey through Moray. Here we look through the **93** old railway arch up Seafield Street towards the town centre.

94 You can feel the chill in this picture, taken on a windy spring day looking over Cullen Bay from the east.

These rocky remnants frame Cullen beach as an explosion of cumulus clouds bubbles up over the **95** town. The coastline continues of course, but that takes us into the territory of another journey …

Published 2011 by Ness Publishing, 47 Academy Street, Elgin, Moray, IV30 1LR

Phone 01343 549663   www.nesspublishing.co.uk   (First edition published in 2008 entitled *Moray: a pictorial souvenir*)

All photographs © Colin and Eithne Nutt except p.1 © Gordon Jones; p.17 © Ballindalloch Castle;
p.20 © Diageo; pp.24/25 & 91 © Scotavia Images; p.39 © Charlie Phillips; p.61 © Gordonstoun School;
p.83 (left) © Keith & Dufftown Railway

Text © Colin Nutt
ISBN 978-1-906549-32-9

Front cover: Telford's Bridge over the Spey at Craigellachie; p.1: a Tornado from RAF Lossiemouth;
p.4: looking out of Auchindoun Castle; this page: massed bands at Forres Highland Games;
back cover: spring on the Spey, Aberlour

For a list of websites and phone numbers please turn over > > > >

Websites and phone numbers (where available) in the order they appear in this book:

Moray: www.thisismoray.com
Speyside: www.greaterspeyside.com
Lossiemouth: www.lossiemouth.org
Cairngorms National Park Authority: www.cairngorms.co.uk
Sueno's Stone: www.historic-scotland.gov.uk (T) 01667460232
Tomintoul: www.visittomintoul.co.uk
Lecht 2090: www.lecht.co.uk (T) 01975 651426
Glenlivet Distillery: www.theglenlivet.com (T) 01340 821720
The Malt Whisky Trail: www.maltwhiskytrail.com (T) 01343 542666
Glen Livet Crown Estate: www.glenlivetestate.co.uk (T) 01479 870070
Grantown-on-Spey: www.grantownonline.co.uk
Revack Estate: Revack Lodge, Grantown-on-Spey, PH26 3NH (T) Tel:01479 872234
Ballindalloch Castle: www.ballindallochcastle.co.uk (T) 01807 500205
Speyside Way: www.moray.gov.uk (T) 01340 881474
Cardhu Distillery: www.diageo.com (T) 01340 872555
Glenfarclas Distillery: www.glenfarclas.co.uk (T) 01807 500257
Ben Rinnes: www.speyside.moray.org/Aberlour/FoBR (T) 01340 871504
Archiestown: www.archiestown.com
Aberlour: www.speyside.moray.org/Aberlour
Speyside Cooperage: www.speysidecooperage.co.uk (T) 01340 871108
Rothes: www.speyside.moray.org/Rothes-on-Spey
Glen Grant Distillery: www.glengrant.com (T) 01340 832103
Baxters: www.baxters.com (T) 01343 820393
Fochabers: www.fochabers-heritage.org.uk
Whale & Dolphin Conservation Society: www.wdcs.org (T) 01343 820339